D1317902

This journal belongs to

....

Date

....

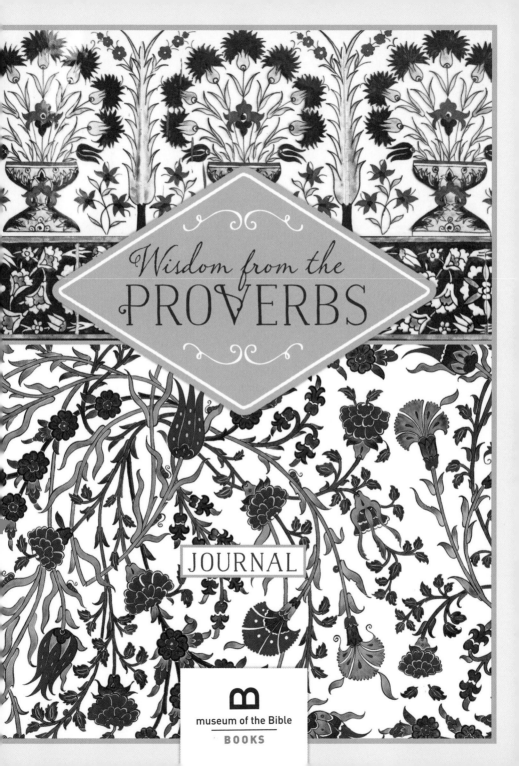

Wisdom from the
PROVERBS

JOURNAL

B
museum of the Bible
BOOKS

Ellie Claire® Gift & Paper Expressions Franklin, TN 37067 | EllieClaire.com
Ellie Claire is a registered trademark of Worthy Media, Inc.

Wisdom from the Proverbs Journal
© 2017 by The Museum of the Bible, Inc.
Published by Ellie Claire, an imprint of Worthy Publishing Group, a division of Worthy Media, Inc.
Published in association with the Museum of the Bible | museumofthebible.org

ISBN 978-1-945470-21-9

All rights reserved. No part of this book may be reproduced in any form, except for brief quotations in printed reviews, without permission in writing from the publisher.

Scripture quotations are taken from the following sources: The Holy Bible, King James Version (KJV). The Holy Bible, New International Version®, NIV® Copyright © 1973, 1978, 1984, 2011 by Biblica, Inc.® All rights reserved worldwide. The Holy Bible, New King James Version® (NKJV). Copyright © 1982 by Thomas Nelson, Inc. The Holy Bible, English Standard Version® (ESV®), copyright © 2001 by Crossway Bibles, a publishing ministry of Good News Publishers. Complete Jewish Bible (CJB), Copyright © 1998 by David H. Stern. All rights reserved. The Holy Scriptures according to the Masoretic Text, a new translation, Jewish Publication Society (JPS), 1917.

Stock or custom editions of Ellie Claire titles may be purchased in bulk for educational, business, ministry, fund-raising, or sales promotional use. For information, please e-mail info@EllieClaire.com.

Art by istockphoto.com

Compiled by Jill Jones
Cover and interior design by Melissa Reagan
Typesetting by Jeff Jansen | AestheticSoup.net

Printed in China

1 2 3 4 5 6 7 8 9 – RRD – 21 20 19 18 17 16

Some books are considered classics. They have "stickiness." Their words not only stick with you after you finish them, but they have had the same effect on many generations before you. In part, this is why the Bible is the most published book in history, and one of the most popular sections in it is the book of Proverbs.

Readers often pause and reflect on its pithy sayings that address everyday problems and situations in memorable ways. Its adages frequently contrast wisdom and folly, reflecting the essence of its name, "Proverbs," from the Hebrew verb *mashal* (meaning "to compare"). These adages have become part of everyday language. That's one of the reasons we find ourselves picking it up again and again.

What better book to spend time with while journaling?

Many Bible studies will work sequentially through a specific biblical book, but will also include regular sections on Proverbs. Part of this is because Proverbs's stand-alone pieces of advice are easily incorporated into common English usage. You're likely aware of many of these, but perhaps you didn't realize their source: "A soft answer turns away wrath" (15:1 NKJV); "Pride goes before destruction" (16:18 NKJV); "A friend loves at all times" (17:17 NKJV); "A cheerful heart is good medicine" (17:22 NIV); and "There is a friend who sticks closer than a brother" (18:24 NIV).

The book of Proverbs promotes what it considers wise and discerning behavior while addressing many of the challenges and tough decisions people face in their daily lives. That's why many of us love it. Actually, through the years, billions of people have loved it. It employs literary tools and techniques to make its teachings noteworthy and compelling. Although compiled in ancient times, in a very different society and culture from our own, this book has been a favorite of people the world over. Based on this popularity, it appears that its content is indeed among the best from ancient history—with sagacious advice to cause each of us to pause and reflect.

One of my favorite proverbs is "As iron sharpens iron, so one person sharpens another" (27:17 NIV). Regardless of its original source, whether gleaned from an ancient culture, Solomon, or another sage, the biblical text has offered the world a gem. Using the prompts included in this journal, I could fill various pages on this one verse. And that's the beauty of Proverbs—its message resonates with the human condition, whether you are looking inward, looking outward to other people, or reflecting on a cause greater than yourself.

Jerry Pattengale

Executive Director of Education, Museum of the Bible (DC);
University Professor, Indiana Wesleyan University

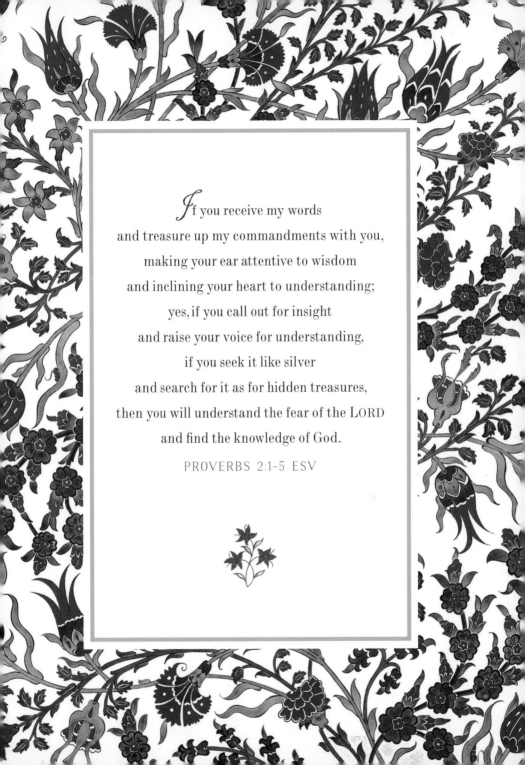

*I*f you receive my words
and treasure up my commandments with you,
making your ear attentive to wisdom
and inclining your heart to understanding;
yes, if you call out for insight
and raise your voice for understanding,
if you seek it like silver
and search for it as for hidden treasures,
then you will understand the fear of the LORD
and find the knowledge of God.

PROVERBS 2:1-5 ESV

Adonai gives wisdom;

from his mouth comes knowledge and understanding.

He…is a shield to those whose conduct is blameless,

in order to guard the courses of justice

and preserve the way of those faithful to him.

Then you will understand righteousness, justice,

fairness and every good path.

For wisdom will enter your heart,

knowledge will be enjoyable for you,

discretion will watch over you,

and discernment will guard you.

PROVERBS 2:6-11 CJB

What does it mean? ....

....

....

....

....

....

....

How does it make me feel? ....

....

....

....

....

....

....

How does it apply to me? ....

....

....

....

....

....

....

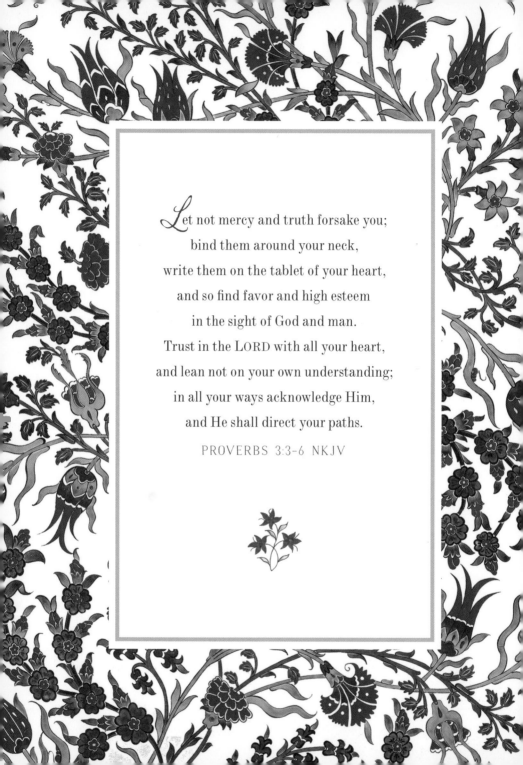

Let not mercy and truth forsake you;
bind them around your neck,
write them on the tablet of your heart,
and so find favor and high esteem
in the sight of God and man.
Trust in the LORD with all your heart,
and lean not on your own understanding;
in all your ways acknowledge Him,
and He shall direct your paths.

PROVERBS 3:3-6 NKJV

What does it mean? ....

....

....

....

....

....

....

....

How does it make me feel? ....

....

....

....

....

....

....

....

How does it apply to me? ....

....

....

....

....

....

....

....

*M*y son, let not them depart from thine eyes;

keep sound wisdom and discretion;

So shall they be life unto thy soul,

and grace to thy neck.

Then shalt thou walk in thy way securely,

and thou shalt not dash thy foot.

When thou liest down, thou shalt not be afraid;

yea, thou shalt lie down, and thy sleep shall be sweet.

PROVERBS 3:21-24 JPS

What does it mean? ....

....

....

....

....

....

....

....

How does it make me feel? ....

....

....

....

....

....

....

....

How does it apply to me? ....

....

....

....

....

....

....

....

*L*et your heart treasure my words;

keep my commands, and live;

gain wisdom, gain insight.

The beginning of wisdom is: get wisdom!

And along with all your getting, get insight!

Cherish her, and she will exalt you;

embrace her, and she will bring you honor;

she will give your head a garland of grace,

bestow on you a crown of glory.

PROVERBS 4:4-5, 7-9 CJB

What does it mean? ....
....
....
....
....
....
....
....

How does it make me feel? ....
....
....
....
....
....
....
....

How does it apply to me? ....
....
....
....
....
....
....
....

$\mathcal{B}$e attentive to my words;
incline your ear to my sayings.
Let them not escape from your sight;
keep them within your heart.
For they are life to those who find them,
and healing to all their flesh.
Keep your heart with all vigilance,
for from it flow the springs of life.

PROVERBS 4:20-23 ESV

What does it mean? ....

....

....

....

....

....

....

....

How does it make me feel? ....

....

....

....

....

....

....

How does it apply to me? ....

....

....

....

....

....

....

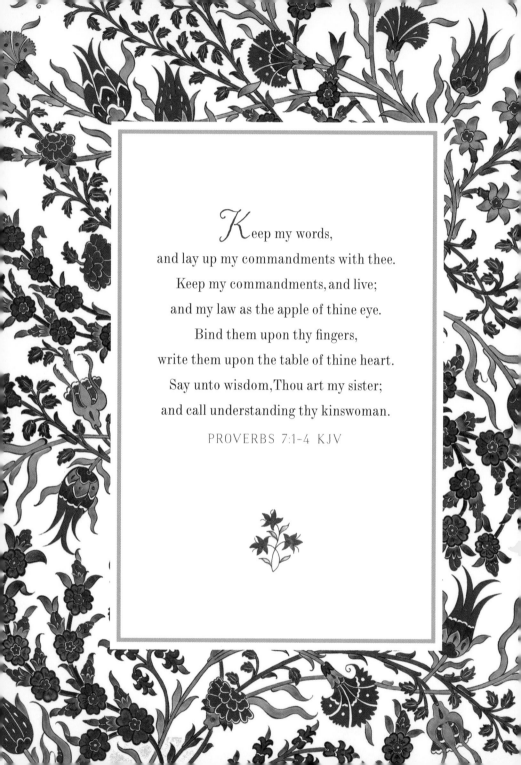

$\mathcal{K}$eep my words,
and lay up my commandments with thee.
Keep my commandments, and live;
and my law as the apple of thine eye.
Bind them upon thy fingers,
write them upon the table of thine heart.
Say unto wisdom, Thou art my sister;
and call understanding thy kinswoman.

PROVERBS 7:1-4 KJV

What does it mean?

How does it make me feel?

How does it apply to me?

*W*isdom is more precious than rubies,
and nothing you desire can compare with her.
"I, wisdom, dwell together with prudence;
I possess knowledge and discretion.
Counsel and sound judgment are mine;
I have insight, I have power.
I love those who love me,
and those who seek me find me.
With me are riches and honor,
enduring wealth and prosperity."

PROVERBS 8:11-12, 14, 17-18 NIV

What does it mean? ....

....

....

....

....

....

....

....

How does it make me feel? ....

....

....

....

....

....

....

....

How does it apply to me? ....

....

....

....

....

....

....

....

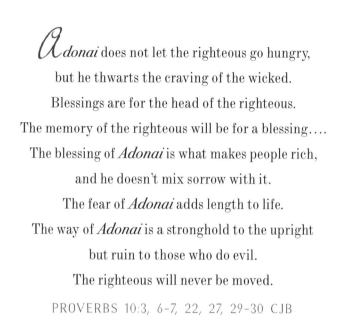

Adonai does not let the righteous go hungry,

but he thwarts the craving of the wicked.

Blessings are for the head of the righteous.

The memory of the righteous will be for a blessing....

The blessing of *Adonai* is what makes people rich,

and he doesn't mix sorrow with it.

The fear of *Adonai* adds length to life.

The way of *Adonai* is a stronghold to the upright

but ruin to those who do evil.

The righteous will never be moved.

PROVERBS 10:3, 6-7, 22, 27, 29-30 CJB

What does it mean? ....
....
....
....
....
....
....
....

How does it make me feel? ....
....
....
....
....
....
....

How does it apply to me? ....
....
....
....
....
....
....
....

The mouth of the righteous is a fountain of life;
but the mouth of the wicked concealeth violence.
Hatred stirreth up strifes;
but love covereth all transgressions.
In the lips of him that hath discernment wisdom is found.
Wise men lay up knowledge,
but the mouth of the foolish is an imminent ruin.
He is in the way of life that heedeth instruction;
but he that forsaketh reproof erreth.

PROVERBS 10:11-14, 17 JPS

What does it mean? ....

....

....

....

....

....

....

....

How does it make me feel? ....

....

....

....

....

....

....

....

How does it apply to me? ....

....

....

....

....

....

....

....

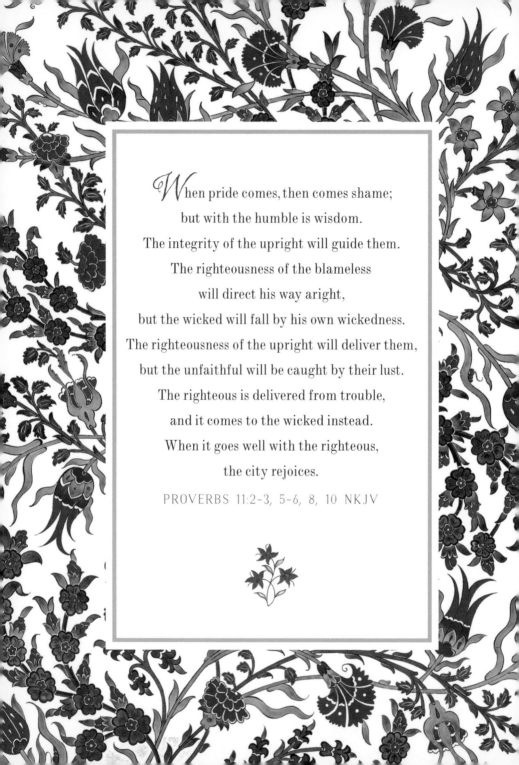

When pride comes, then comes shame;

but with the humble is wisdom.

The integrity of the upright will guide them.

The righteousness of the blameless

will direct his way aright,

but the wicked will fall by his own wickedness.

The righteousness of the upright will deliver them,

but the unfaithful will be caught by their lust.

The righteous is delivered from trouble,

and it comes to the wicked instead.

When it goes well with the righteous,

the city rejoices.

PROVERBS 11:2-3, 5-6, 8, 10 NKJV

What does it mean?

How does it make me feel?

How does it apply to me?

$\mathscr{B}$y the blessing of the upright a city is exalted,
but by the mouth of the wicked it is overthrown.
Whoever belittles his neighbor lacks sense,
but a man of understanding remains silent.
Whoever goes about slandering reveals secrets,
but he who is trustworthy in spirit keeps a thing covered.
Where there is no guidance, a people falls,
but in an abundance of counselors there is safety.

PROVERBS 11:11-14 ESV

What does it mean? ....
....
....
....
....
....
....
....

How does it make me feel? ....
....
....
....
....
....
....
....

How does it apply to me? ....
....
....
....
....
....
....
....

$\mathcal{S}$ome give freely and still get richer,

while others are stingy but grow still poorer.

The person who blesses others will prosper;

he who satisfies others will be satisfied himself.

The people will curse him who withholds grain;

but if he sells it, blessings will be on his head.

He who strives for good obtains favor,

but he who searches for evil—it comes to him!

He who trusts in his riches will fall,

but the righteous will flourish like sprouting leaves.

PROVERBS 11:24-28 CJB

What does it mean? ....
....
....
....
....
....
....

How does it make me feel? ....
....
....
....
....
....
....

How does it apply to me? ....
....
....
....
....
....
....

Whoever loves instruction loves knowledge,
but he who hates correction is stupid.
A good man obtains favor from the LORD,
but a man of wicked intentions He will condemn.
A man is not established by wickedness,
but the root of the righteous cannot be moved.
The thoughts of the righteous are right,
but the counsels of the wicked are deceitful.
The wicked are overthrown and are no more,
but the house of the righteous will stand.

PROVERBS 12:1-3, 5, 7 NKJV

What does it mean? ....
....
....
....
....
....
....
....

How does it make me feel? ....
....
....
....
....
....
....
....

How does it apply to me? ....
....
....
....
....
....
....
....

$\mathcal{A}$ righteous man regardeth the life of his beast:
but the tender mercies of the wicked are cruel.
He that tilleth his land shall be satisfied with bread:
but he that followeth vain persons
is void of understanding.
The wicked desireth the net of evil men:
but the root of the righteous yieldeth fruit.
A man shall be satisfied with good
by the fruit of his mouth:
and the recompence of a man's hands
shall be rendered unto him.

PROVERBS 12:10-12, 14 KJV

What does it mean? ....

....

....

....

....

....

....

....

How does it make me feel? ....

....

....

....

....

....

....

....

How does it apply to me? ....

....

....

....

....

....

....

....

*T*hose who promote peace have joy.
No harm overtakes the righteous,
but the wicked have their fill of trouble.
The LORD detests lying lips,
but he delights in people who are trustworthy.
The prudent keep their knowledge to themselves,
but a fool's heart blurts out folly.
Diligent hands will rule,
but laziness ends in forced labor.
Anxiety weighs down the heart,
but a kind word cheers it up.

PROVERBS 12:20-25 NIV

What does it mean? ....

....

....

....

....

....

....

....

How does it make me feel? ....

....

....

....

....

....

....

How does it apply to me? ....

....

....

....

....

....

....

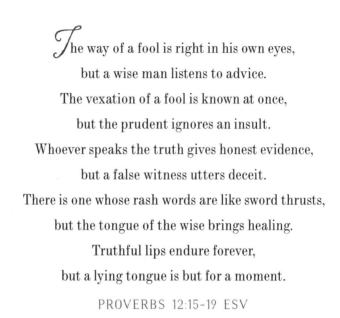

The way of a fool is right in his own eyes,

but a wise man listens to advice.

The vexation of a fool is known at once,

but the prudent ignores an insult.

Whoever speaks the truth gives honest evidence,

but a false witness utters deceit.

There is one whose rash words are like sword thrusts,

but the tongue of the wise brings healing.

Truthful lips endure forever,

but a lying tongue is but for a moment.

PROVERBS 12:15-19 ESV

What does it mean? ....
....
....
....
....
....
....
....

How does it make me feel? ....
....
....
....
....
....
....

How does it apply to me? ....
....
....
....
....
....
....
....

A lazy man doesn't roast what he hunted;
but when a man is diligent, his wealth is precious.
A son who heeds his father's discipline is wise,
but a scoffer doesn't listen to rebuke.
A [good] man enjoys good as a result of what he says,
but the essence of the treacherous is violence.
He who guards his mouth preserves his life,
but one who talks too much comes to ruin.
The lazy person wants but doesn't have;
the diligent get their desires filled.

PROVERBS 12:27; 13:1-4 CJB

What does it mean? ....
....
....
....
....
....
....
....

How does it make me feel? ....
....
....
....
....
....
....
....

How does it apply to me? ....
....
....
....
....
....
....
....

$\mathcal{R}$ighteousness protects him
whose way is honest,
but wickedness brings down the sinner.
There are those with nothing
who pretend they are rich,
also those with great wealth
who pretend they are poor.
Insolence produces only strife,
but wisdom is found with those who take advice.
Hope deferred makes the heart sick,
but desire fulfilled is a tree of life.

PROVERBS 13:6-7, 10, 12 NKJV

What does it mean? ....
....
....
....
....
....
....
....

How does it make me feel? ....
....
....
....
....
....
....
....

How does it apply to me? ....
....
....
....
....
....
....
....

*W*hoever despises the word brings destruction on himself,
but he who reveres the commandment will be rewarded.
The teaching of the wise is a fountain of life,
that one may turn away from the snares of death.
Poverty and disgrace come to him who ignores instruction,
but whoever heeds reproof is honored.
A desire fulfilled is sweet to the soul,
but to turn away from evil is an abomination to fools.
Whoever walks with the wise becomes wise,
but the companion of fools will suffer harm.

PROVERBS 13:13-14, 18-20 ESV

What does it mean? ....

....

....

....

....

....

....

....

How does it make me feel? ....

....

....

....

....

....

....

How does it apply to me? ....

....

....

....

....

....

....

$\mathcal{A}$n honest witness will not lie,

but a false witness lies with every breath.

A scoffer seeks wisdom in vain,

but knowledge comes easily to someone with discernment.

The wisdom of the cautious makes him know where he is going,

but the folly of fools misleads them.

Guilt offerings make a mockery of fools;

but among the upright there is good will.

PROVERBS 14:5-6, 8-9 CJB

What does it mean? ....

....

....

....

....

....

....

....

How does it make me feel? ....

....

....

....

....

....

....

How does it apply to me? ....

....

....

....

....

....

....

....

The heart knows its own bitterness,

and no stranger can share its joy.

The house of the wicked will be destroyed,

but the tent of the upright will flourish.

There can be a way which seems right to a person,

but at its end are the ways of death.

Even in laughter the heart can be sad,

and joy may end in sorrow.

A backslider is filled up with his own ways,

but a good person gets satisfaction from himself.

PROVERBS 14:10-14 NKJV

What does it mean? ....
....
....
....
....
....
....
....
....

How does it make me feel? ....
....
....
....
....
....
....
....

How does it apply to me? ....
....
....
....
....
....
....
....

The simple believes everything,

but the prudent gives thought to his steps.

One who is wise is cautious

and turns away from evil,

but a fool is reckless and careless.

Whoever despises his neighbor is a sinner,

but blessed is he who is generous to the poor.

Do they not go astray who devise evil?

Those who devise good meet

steadfast love and faithfulness.

In all toil there is profit,

but mere talk tends only to poverty.

PROVERBS 14:15-16, 21-23 ESV

What does it mean? ....

....

....

....

....

....

....

....

How does it make me feel? ....

....

....

....

....

....

....

....

How does it apply to me? ....

....

....

....

....

....

....

....

*I*n the fear of the LORD is strong confidence:
and his children shall have a place of refuge.
The fear of the LORD is a fountain of life,
to depart from the snares of death.
He that is slow to wrath is of great understanding:
but he that is hasty of spirit exalteth folly.
A sound heart is the life of the flesh:
but envy the rottenness of the bones.

PROVERBS 14:26-27, 29-30 KJV

What does it mean? ....
....
....
....
....
....
....
....

How does it make me feel? ....
....
....
....
....
....
....
....

How does it apply to me? ....
....
....
....
....
....
....
....

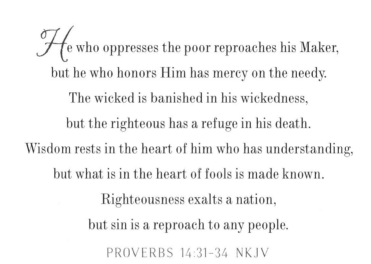

He who oppresses the poor reproaches his Maker,
but he who honors Him has mercy on the needy.
The wicked is banished in his wickedness,
but the righteous has a refuge in his death.
Wisdom rests in the heart of him who has understanding,
but what is in the heart of fools is made known.
Righteousness exalts a nation,
but sin is a reproach to any people.

PROVERBS 14:31-34 NKJV

What does it mean?

How does it make me feel?

How does it apply to me?

A gentle response deflects fury,
but a harsh word makes tempers rise.
The tongue of the wise presents knowledge well,
but the mouth of a fool spews out folly.
The eyes of *Adonai* are everywhere,
watching the evil and the good.
A soothing tongue is a tree of life,
but when it twists things, it breaks the spirit.

PROVERBS 15:1-4 CJB

What does it mean? ....

....
....
....
....
....
....
....

How does it make me feel? ....

....
....
....
....
....
....
....

How does it apply to me? ....

....
....
....
....
....
....
....

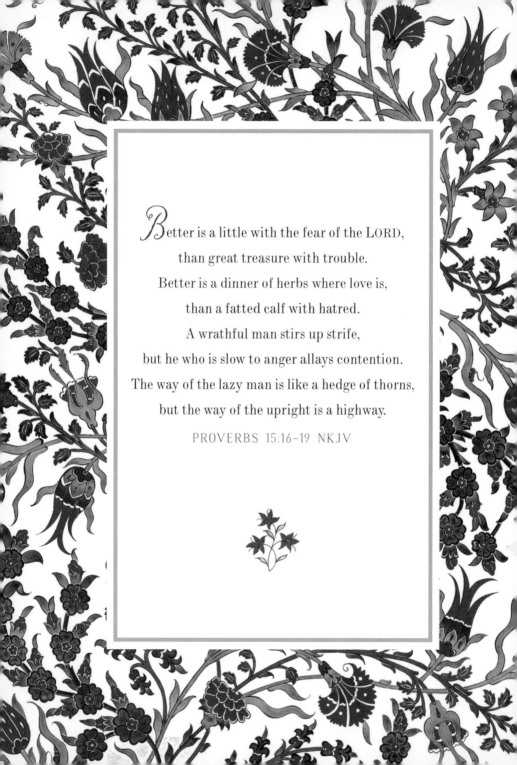

*B*etter is a little with the fear of the L ORD,
than great treasure with trouble.
Better is a dinner of herbs where love is,
than a fatted calf with hatred.
A wrathful man stirs up strife,
but he who is slow to anger allays contention.
The way of the lazy man is like a hedge of thorns,
but the way of the upright is a highway.

PROVERBS 15:16–19 NKJV

What does it mean?

How does it make me feel?

How does it apply to me?

In the house of the righteous there is much treasure,

but trouble befalls the income of the wicked.

The lips of the wise spread knowledge;

not so the hearts of fools.

A glad heart makes a cheerful face,

but by sorrow of heart the spirit is crushed.

The heart of him who has understanding seeks knowledge,

but the mouths of fools feed on folly.

All the days of the afflicted are evil,

but the cheerful of heart has a continual feast.

PROVERBS 15:6-7, 13-15 ESV

What does it mean? ....
....
....
....
....
....
....
....

How does it make me feel? ....
....
....
....
....
....
....
....

How does it apply to me? ....
....
....
....
....
....
....
....

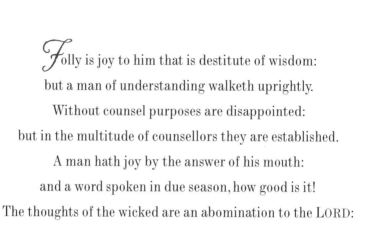

*F*olly is joy to him that is destitute of wisdom:

but a man of understanding walketh uprightly.

Without counsel purposes are disappointed:

but in the multitude of counsellors they are established.

A man hath joy by the answer of his mouth:

and a word spoken in due season, how good is it!

The thoughts of the wicked are an abomination to the LORD:

but the words of the pure are pleasant words.

PROVERBS 15:21-23, 26 KJV

What does it mean? ....

....

....

....

....

....

....

....

....

How does it make me feel? ....

....

....

....

....

....

....

....

How does it apply to me? ....

....

....

....

....

....

....

....

The heart of the righteous weighs its answers,
but the mouth of the wicked gushes evil.
Light in a messenger's eyes brings joy to the heart,
and good news gives health to the bones.
Whoever heeds life-giving correction
will be at home among the wise.
Those who disregard discipline despise themselves,
but the one who heeds correction gains understanding.
Wisdom's instruction is to fear the LORD,
and humility comes before honor.

PROVERBS 15:28, 30-33 NIV

What does it mean? ....

....

....

....

....

....

....

....

How does it make me feel? ....

....

....

....

....

....

....

....

How does it apply to me? ....

....

....

....

....

....

....

....

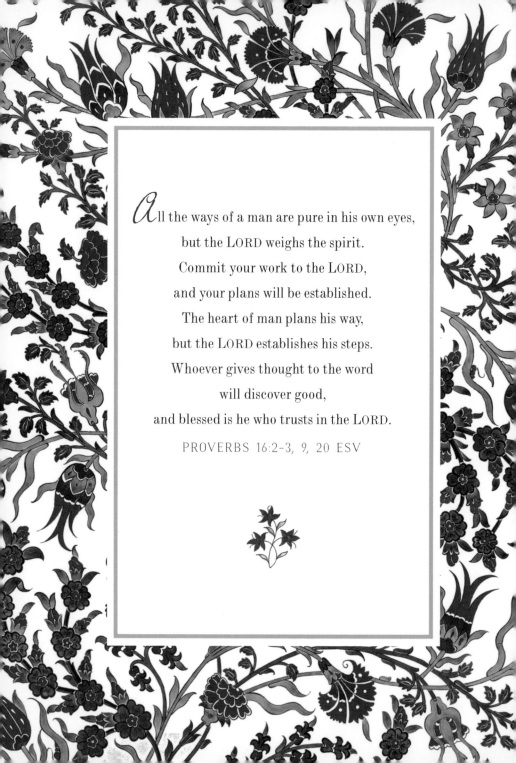

$\mathcal{A}$ll the ways of a man are pure in his own eyes,
but the LORD weighs the spirit.
Commit your work to the LORD,
and your plans will be established.
The heart of man plans his way,
but the LORD establishes his steps.
Whoever gives thought to the word
will discover good,
and blessed is he who trusts in the LORD.

PROVERBS 16:2-3, 9, 20 ESV

What does it mean? ....

....

....

....

....

....

....

....

How does it make me feel? ....

....

....

....

....

....

....

....

How does it apply to me? ....

....

....

....

....

....

....

....

The wise in heart will be called prudent,

and sweetness of the lips increases learning.

Understanding is a wellspring of life to him who has it.

But the correction of fools is folly.

The heart of the wise teaches his mouth,

and adds learning to his lips.

Pleasant words are like a honeycomb,

sweetness to the soul and health to the bones.

There is a way that seems right to a man,

but its end is the way of death.

PROVERBS 16:21-25 NKJV

What does it mean?

....

....

....

....

....

....

....

....

How does it make me feel?

....

....

....

....

....

....

....

....

How does it apply to me?

....

....

....

....

....

....

....

....

A working man's appetite acts on his behalf,
because his hunger presses him on.
A deceitful person stirs up strife,
and a slanderer can separate even close friends.
White hair is a crown of honor
obtained by righteous living.
He who controls his temper is better than a war hero,
he who rules his spirit better than he who captures a city.
One can cast lots into one's lap,
but the decision comes from *Adonai*.

PROVERBS 16:26, 28, 31-33 CJB

What does it mean? ....

....
....
....
....
....
....
....

How does it make me feel? ....

....
....
....
....
....
....
....

How does it apply to me? ....

....
....
....
....
....
....
....

*B*etter is a dry morsel and quietness therewith,

than a house full of feasting with strife.

The refining pot is for silver, and the furnace for gold;

but the LORD trieth the hearts.

A evil-doer giveth heed to wicked lips;

and a liar giveth ear to a mischievous tongue.

Children's children are the crown of old men;

And the glory of children are their fathers.

PROVERBS 17:1, 3-4, 6 JPS

What does it mean?

....

....

....

....

....

....

....

....

How does it make me feel?

....

....

....

....

....

....

....

....

How does it apply to me?

....

....

....

....

....

....

....

....

Whoever covers an offense seeks love,
but he who repeats a matter separates close friends.
A rebuke goes deeper into a man of understanding
than a hundred blows into a fool.
The beginning of strife is like letting out water,
so quit before the quarrel breaks out.
A friend loves at all times,
and a brother is born for adversity.

PROVERBS 17:9-10, 14, 17 ESV

What does it mean? ....
....
....
....
....
....
....
....

How does it make me feel? ....
....
....
....
....
....
....

How does it apply to me? ....
....
....
....
....
....
....

$\mathcal{A}$ merry heart does good, like medicine,

but a broken spirit dries the bones.

Wisdom is in the sight of him who has understanding,

but the eyes of a fool are on the ends of the earth.

Also, to punish the righteous is not good,

nor to strike princes for their uprightness.

He who has knowledge spares his words,

and a man of understanding is of a calm spirit.

Even a fool is counted wise when he holds his peace;

when he shuts his lips, he is considered perceptive.

PROVERBS 17:22, 24, 26-28 NKJV

What does it mean? ....

....

....

....

....

....

....

....

How does it make me feel? ....

....

....

....

....

....

....

How does it apply to me? ....

....

....

....

....

....

....

$\mathcal{A}$ fool takes no pleasure in trying to understand;

he only wants to express his own opinion.

The words of a man's mouth are deep water,

a gushing torrent, a fountain of wisdom.

It is not good to be partial to the guilty

and thus deprive the innocent of justice.

Whoever is lazy in doing his work

is brother to the destroyer.

PROVERBS 18:2, 4-5, 9 CJB

What does it mean? ....
....
....
....
....
....
....
....

How does it make me feel? ....
....
....
....
....
....
....
....

How does it apply to me? ....
....
....
....
....
....
....
....

The name of the LORD is a fortified tower;
the righteous run to it and are safe.
The wealth of the rich is their fortified city;
they imagine it a wall too high to scale.
Before a downfall the heart is haughty,
but humility comes before honor.
To answer before listening—
that is folly and shame.
The human spirit can endure in sickness,
but a crushed spirit who can bear?

PROVERBS 18:10-14 NIV

What does it mean? ....

....

....

....

....

....

....

....

How does it make me feel? ....

....

....

....

....

....

....

How does it apply to me? ....

....

....

....

....

....

....

....

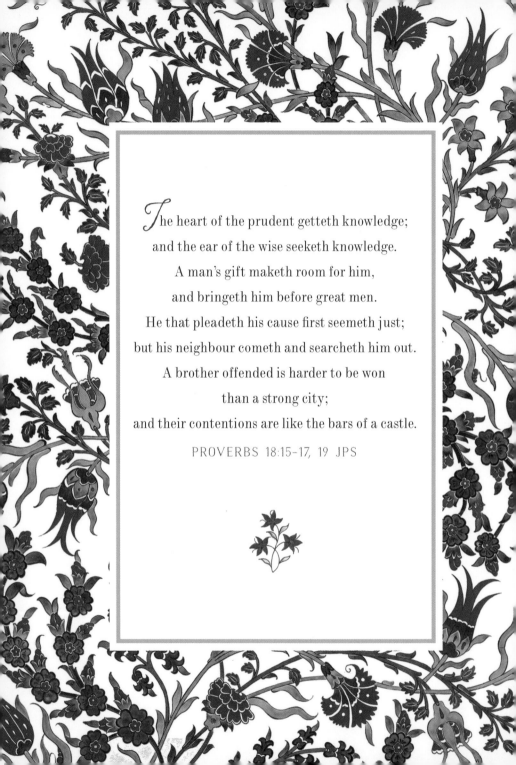

The heart of the prudent getteth knowledge;
and the ear of the wise seeketh knowledge.
A man's gift maketh room for him,
and bringeth him before great men.
He that pleadeth his cause first seemeth just;
but his neighbour cometh and searcheth him out.
A brother offended is harder to be won
than a strong city;
and their contentions are like the bars of a castle.

PROVERBS 18:15–17, 19 JPS

What does it mean? ....
....
....
....
....
....
....
....
....

How does it make me feel? ....
....
....
....
....
....
....
....
....

How does it apply to me? ....
....
....
....
....
....
....
....
....

$\mathcal{A}$ man's stomach shall be satisfied from the fruit of his mouth;

from the produce of his lips he shall be filled.

Death and life are in the power of the tongue,

and those who love it will eat its fruit.

He who finds a wife finds a good thing,

and obtains favor from the LORD.

A man who has friends must himself be friendly,

but there is a friend who sticks closer than a brother.

PROVERBS 18:20-22, 24 NKJV

What does it mean? ....

....

....

....

....

....

....

....

How does it make me feel? ....

....

....

....

....

....

....

....

How does it apply to me? ....

....

....

....

....

....

....

....

$\mathcal{B}$etter is a poor person who walks in his integrity
than one who is crooked in speech and is a fool.
Desire without knowledge is not good,
and whoever makes haste with his feet misses his way.
When a man's folly brings his way to ruin,
his heart rages against the LORD.
Wealth brings many new friends,
but a poor man is deserted by his friend.
A false witness will not go unpunished,
and he who breathes out lies will not escape.

PROVERBS 19:1-5 ESV

What does it mean? ....
....
....
....
....
....
....
....

How does it make me feel? ....
....
....
....
....
....
....
....

How does it apply to me? ....
....
....
....
....
....
....
....

Many will intreat the favour of the prince:
and every man is a friend to him that giveth gifts.

All the brethren of the poor do hate him:
how much more do his friends go far from him?

He that getteth wisdom loveth his own soul:
he that keepeth understanding shall find good.

A false witness shall not be unpunished,
and he that speaketh lies shall perish.

PROVERBS 19:6-9 KJV

What does it mean? ....
....
....
....
....
....
....
....

How does it make me feel? ....
....
....
....
....
....
....
....

How does it apply to me? ....
....
....
....
....
....
....
....

People with good sense are slow to anger,
and it is their glory to overlook an offense.
A king's wrath is like the roaring of a lion,
but his favor is like dew on the grass.
A son who is a fool is his father's ruin,
and a nagging wife is like a leak that keeps dripping.
Laziness makes people fall asleep,
and an idle person will go hungry.

PROVERBS 19:11-13, 15 CJB

What does it mean? ....

....

....

....

....

....

....

....

How does it make me feel? ....

....

....

....

....

....

....

....

How does it apply to me? ....

....

....

....

....

....

....

....

*H*e who keeps the commandment keeps his soul,

but he who is careless of his ways will die.

He who has pity on the poor lends to the LORD,

and He will pay back what he has given.

A man of great wrath will suffer punishment;

for if you rescue him, you will have to do it again.

Listen to counsel and receive instruction,

that you may be wise in your latter days.

PROVERBS 19:16-17, 19-20 NKJV

What does it mean? ....

....

....

....

....

....

....

....

How does it make me feel? ....

....

....

....

....

....

....

....

How does it apply to me? ....

....

....

....

....

....

....

....

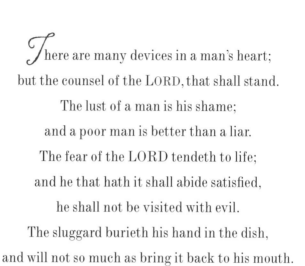

There are many devices in a man's heart;

but the counsel of the LORD, that shall stand.

The lust of a man is his shame;

and a poor man is better than a liar.

The fear of the LORD tendeth to life;

and he that hath it shall abide satisfied,

he shall not be visited with evil.

The sluggard burieth his hand in the dish,

and will not so much as bring it back to his mouth.

PROVERBS 19:21-24 JPS

What does it mean? ....

....

....

....

....

....

....

....

How does it make me feel? ....

....

....

....

....

....

....

....

How does it apply to me? ....

....

....

....

....

....

....

....

Strike a scoffer, and the simple will learn prudence;
reprove a man of understanding, and he will gain knowledge.
Cease to hear instruction, my son,
and you will stray from the words of knowledge.
It is an honor for a man to keep aloof from strife,
but every fool will be quarreling.
The sluggard does not plow in the autumn;
he will seek at harvest and have nothing.

PROVERBS 19:25, 27; 20:3-4 ESV

What does it mean?

....

....

....

....

....

....

....

How does it make me feel?

....

....

....

....

....

....

....

How does it apply to me?

....

....

....

....

....

....

....

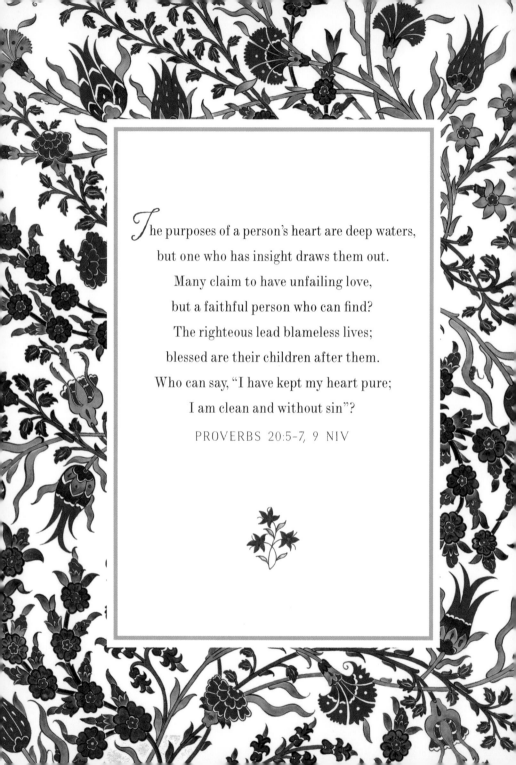

The purposes of a person's heart are deep waters,
but one who has insight draws them out.
Many claim to have unfailing love,
but a faithful person who can find?
The righteous lead blameless lives;
blessed are their children after them.
Who can say, "I have kept my heart pure;
I am clean and without sin"?

PROVERBS 20:5-7, 9 NIV

What does it mean?

How does it make me feel?

How does it apply to me?

$\mathscr{E}$ven a child is known by his doings,

whether his work be pure, and whether it be right.

The hearing ear, and the seeing eye,

the LORD hath made even both of them.

Love not sleep, lest thou come to poverty;

open thine eyes, and thou shalt be satisfied with bread.

There is gold, and a multitude of rubies:

but the lips of knowledge are a precious jewel.

PROVERBS 20:11-13, 15 KJV

What does it mean? ....

....

....

....

....

....

....

....

How does it make me feel? ....

....

....

....

....

....

....

....

How does it apply to me? ....

....

....

....

....

....

....

....

A man's steps are from the LORD;

how then can man understand his way?

The spirit of man is the lamp of the LORD,

searching all his innermost parts.

Steadfast love and faithfulness preserve the king,

and by steadfast love his throne is upheld.

The glory of young men is their strength,

but the splendor of old men is their gray hair.

PROVERBS 20:24, 27-29 ESV

What does it mean? ....

....

....

....

....

....

....

....

How does it make me feel? ....

....

....

....

....

....

....

....

How does it apply to me? ....

....

....

....

....

....

....

....

*B*read gained by deceit is sweet to a man,

but afterward his mouth will be filled with gravel.

Plans are established by counsel;

by wise counsel wage war.

He who goes about as a talebearer reveals secrets;

therefore do not associate with one who flatters with his lips.

An inheritance gained hastily at the beginning

will not be blessed at the end.

Do not say,"I will recompense evil";

wait for the LORD, and He will save you.

PROVERBS 20:17-19, 21-22 NKJV

What does it mean?

How does it make me feel?

How does it apply to me?

The king's heart in *Adonai*'s hand
is like streams of water—
he directs it wherever he pleases.
All a person's ways are right in his own view,
but *Adonai* weighs the heart.
To do what is right and just
is more pleasing to *Adonai* than sacrifice.
Haughty looks, a proud heart—
what the wicked plow is sin.
The plans of the diligent lead only to abundance;
but all who rush in arrive only at want.

PROVERBS 21:1-5 CJB

What does it mean?

....

....

....

....

....

....

....

....

How does it make me feel?

....

....

....

....

....

....

....

....

How does it apply to me?

....

....

....

....

....

....

....

....

*T*he way of a guilty man is perverse;

but as for the pure, his work is right.

Better to dwell in a corner of a housetop,

than in a house shared with a contentious woman.

The soul of the wicked desires evil;

his neighbor finds no favor in his eyes.

When the scoffer is punished, the simple is made wise;

but when the wise is instructed, he receives knowledge.

The righteous God wisely considers the house of the wicked,

overthrowing the wicked for their wickedness.

PROVERBS 21:8-12 NKJV

What does it mean? ....
....
....
....
....
....
....
....

How does it make me feel? ....
....
....
....
....
....
....
....

How does it apply to me? ....
....
....
....
....
....
....
....

Whoso stoppeth his ears at the cry of the poor,

he also shall cry himself, but shall not be answered.

A gift in secret pacifieth anger,

and a present in the bosom strong wrath.

To do justly is joy to the righteous,

but ruin to the workers of iniquity.

He that loveth pleasure shall be a poor man;

he that loveth wine…shall not be rich.

PROVERBS 21:13-15, 17 JPS

What does it mean? ....
....
....
....
....
....
....
....

How does it make me feel? ....
....
....
....
....
....
....
....

How does it apply to me? ....
....
....
....
....
....
....
....

*P*recious treasure and oil are in a wise man's dwelling,

but a foolish man devours it.

Whoever pursues righteousness and kindness

will find life, righteousness, and honor.

A wise man scales the city of the mighty

and brings down the stronghold in which they trust.

Whoever keeps his mouth and his tongue

keeps himself out of trouble.

PROVERBS 21:20-23 ESV

What does it mean? ....
....
....
....
....
....
....
....
....

How does it make me feel? ....
....
....
....
....
....
....
....

How does it apply to me? ....
....
....
....
....
....
....
....
....

The craving of a sluggard will be the death of him,
because his hands refuse to work.
All day long he craves for more,
but the righteous give without sparing.
The wicked put up a bold front,
but the upright give thought to their ways.
There is no wisdom, no insight, no plan
that can succeed against the LORD.
The horse is made ready for the day of battle,
but victory rests with the LORD.

PROVERBS 21:25-26, 29-31 NIV

What does it mean? ....

....

....

....

....

....

....

How does it make me feel? ....

....

....

....

....

....

How does it apply to me? ....

....

....

....

....

....

....

$\mathcal{A}$ good name is rather to be chosen than great riches,

and loving favour rather than silver and gold.

The rich and poor meet together:

the LORD is the maker of them all.

A prudent man foreseeth the evil, and hideth himself:

but the simple pass on, and are punished.

By humility and the fear of the LORD

are riches, and honour, and life.

PROVERBS 22:1-4 KJV

What does it mean? ....
....
....
....
....
....
....

How does it make me feel? ....
....
....
....
....
....
....

How does it apply to me? ....
....
....
....
....
....
....

*T*horns and snares are in the way of the perverse;

he who guards his soul will be far from them.

Train up a child in the way he should go,

and when he is old he will not depart from it.

The rich rules over the poor,

and the borrower is servant to the lender.

He who sows iniquity will reap sorrow,

and the rod of his anger will fail.

He who has a generous eye will be blessed,

for he gives of his bread to the poor.

PROVERBS 22:5-9 NKJV

What does it mean? ....

....

....

....

....

....

....

....

How does it make me feel? ....

....

....

....

....

....

....

How does it apply to me? ....

....

....

....

....

....

....

*H*e who loves the pure-hearted and is gracious in speech
will have the king as his friend.
The eyes of *Adonai* protect [the man with] knowledge,
but he overturns the plans of a traitor.
A lazy man says, "There's a lion outside!
I'll be killed if I go out in the street!"
Both oppressing the poor to enrich oneself
and giving to the rich yield only loss.

PROVERBS 22:11-13, 16 CJB

What does it mean?

How does it make me feel?

How does it apply to me?

*I*ncline your ear, and hear the words of the wise,
and apply your heart to my knowledge,
for it will be pleasant if you keep them within you,
if all of them are ready on your lips.
That your trust may be in the LORD,
I have made them known to you today, even to you.
Have I not written for you thirty sayings
of counsel and knowledge,
to make you know what is right and true,
that you may give a true answer to those who sent you?

PROVERBS 22:17-21 ESV

What does it mean? ....

....

....

....

....

....

....

....

How does it make me feel? ....

....

....

....

....

....

....

....

How does it apply to me? ....

....

....

....

....

....

....

....

Do not rob the poor because he is poor,

nor oppress the afflicted at the gate;

For the LORD will plead their cause,

and plunder the soul of those who plunder them.

Make no friendship with an angry man,

and with a furious man do not go,

lest you learn his ways

and set a snare for your soul.

Do you see a man who excels in his work?

He will stand before kings;

he will not stand before unknown men.

PROVERBS 22:22-25, 29 NKJV

What does it mean? ....
....
....
....
....
....
....
....
....

How does it make me feel? ....
....
....
....
....
....
....
....
....

How does it apply to me? ....
....
....
....
....
....
....
....
....

$\mathcal{A}$pply thy heart unto instruction,

and thine ears to the words of knowledge.

My son, if thy heart be wise,

my heart will be glad, even mine;

Let not thy heart envy sinners,

but be in the fear of the LORD all the day;

For surely there is a future;

And thy hope shall not be cut off.

PROVERBS 23:12, 15, 17-18 JPS

What does it mean?

How does it make me feel?

How does it apply to me?

The father of the righteous shall greatly rejoice:
and he that begetteth a wise child shall have joy of him.
Thy father and thy mother shall be glad,
and she that bare thee shall rejoice.
My son, give me thine heart,
and let thine eyes observe my ways.

PROVERBS 23:24-26 KJV

What does it mean? ....

....

....

....

....

....

....

....

How does it make me feel? ....

....

....

....

....

....

....

....

How does it apply to me? ....

....

....

....

....

....

....

....

When you sit down to dine with a ruler,
think carefully about who is before you.
If you have a big appetite,
put a knife to your throat!
Don't be greedy for his delicacies,
for they are deceptive food.
Don't exhaust yourself in pursuit of wealth;
be smart enough to desist.
If you make your eyes rush at it,
it's no longer there!
For wealth will surely grow wings,
like an eagle flying off to the sky.

PROVERBS 23:1-5 CJB

What does it mean? ....

....

....

....

....

....

....

....

How does it make me feel? ....

....

....

....

....

....

....

....

How does it apply to me? ....

....

....

....

....

....

....

....

*H*ear, my son, and be wise,
and direct your heart in the way.
Be not among drunkards
or among gluttonous eaters of meat,
for the drunkard and the glutton will come to poverty,
and slumber will clothe them with rags.
Listen to your father who gave you life,
and do not despise your mother when she is old.
Buy truth, and do not sell it;
buy wisdom, instruction, and understanding.

PROVERBS 23:19-23 ESV

What does it mean? ....
....
....
....
....
....
....
....

How does it make me feel? ....
....
....
....
....
....
....
....

How does it apply to me? ....
....
....
....
....
....
....
....

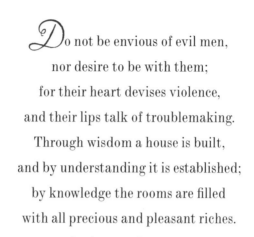

𝒟o not be envious of evil men,

nor desire to be with them;

for their heart devises violence,

and their lips talk of troublemaking.

Through wisdom a house is built,

and by understanding it is established;

by knowledge the rooms are filled

with all precious and pleasant riches.

A wise man is strong,

yes, a man of knowledge increases strength;

for by wise counsel you will wage your own war,

and in a multitude of counselors there is safety.

PROVERBS 24:1-6 NKJV

What does it mean?

How does it make me feel?

How does it apply to me?

*I*f you slack off on a day of distress,
your strength is small indeed.
Yes, rescue those being dragged off to death —
won't you save those about to be killed?
If you say, "We knew nothing about it,"
won't he who weighs hearts discern it?
Yes, he who guards you will know it
and repay each one as his deeds deserve.
My son, eat honey, for it is good....
Know that wisdom is similar[ly sweet] to your soul;
if you find it, then you will have a future,
what you hope for will not be cut off.

PROVERBS 24:10-14 CJB

What does it mean?

How does it make me feel?

How does it apply to me?

$\mathcal{D}$o not rejoice when your enemy falls,
and let not your heart be glad when he stumbles,
lest the LORD see it and be displeased,
and turn away his anger from him.
Fret not yourself because of evildoers,
and be not envious of the wicked,
for the evil man has no future....
My son, fear the LORD and the king,
and do not join with those who do otherwise,
for disaster will arise suddenly from them,
and who knows the ruin that will come
from them both?

PROVERBS 24:17-22 ESV

What does it mean? ....
....
....
....
....
....
....

How does it make me feel? ....
....
....
....
....
....
....

How does it apply to me? ....
....
....
....
....
....
....

$\mathscr{H}$e that saith unto the wicked, Thou are righteous;

him shall the people curse, nations shall abhor him:

But to them that rebuke him shall be delight,

and a good blessing shall come upon them.

Prepare thy work without, and make it fit for thyself in the field;

and afterwards build thine house.

Be not a witness against thy neighbour without cause;

and deceive not with thy lips.

Say not, I will do so to him as he hath done to me:

I will render to the man according to his work.

PROVERBS 24:24-25, 27-29 KJV

What does it mean? ....
....
....
....
....
....
....

How does it make me feel? ....
....
....
....
....
....
....

How does it apply to me? ....
....
....
....
....
....
....

$\mathcal{I}$ went by the field of the lazy man…

and there it was, all overgrown with thorns;

its surface was covered with nettles;

its stone wall was broken down.

When I saw it, I considered it well;

I looked on it and received instruction:

a little sleep, a little slumber,

a little folding of the hands to rest;

so shall your poverty come like a prowler,

and your need like an armed man.

PROVERBS 24:30-34 NKJV

What does it mean?

How does it make me feel?

How does it apply to me?

$\mathcal{L}$ike apples of gold in settings of silver
is a word appropriately spoken.
Like a gold earring, like a fine gold necklace
is a wise reprover to a receptive ear.
Like the coldness of snow in the heat of the harvest
is a faithful messenger to the one who sends him;
he refreshes his master's spirit.
Like clouds and wind that bring no rain
is he who boasts of gifts he never gives.

PROVERBS 25:11-14 CJB

What does it mean? ....

....

....

....

....

....

....

....

How does it make me feel? ....

....

....

....

....

....

....

....

How does it apply to me? ....

....

....

....

....

....

....

....

*B*oast not thyself of to-morrow;

for thou knowest not what a day may bring forth.

Let another man praise thee,

and not thine own mouth;

a stranger, and not thine own lips.

Better is open rebuke

than love that is hidden.

Faithful are the wounds of a friend....

The full soul loatheth a honeycomb;

but to the hungry soul every bitter thing is sweet.

PROVERBS 27:1-2, 5-7 JPS

What does it mean? ....
....
....
....
....
....
....

How does it make me feel? ....
....
....
....
....
....
....

How does it apply to me? ....
....
....
....
....
....
....

*I*f you have found honey, eat only enough for you,

lest you have your fill of it and vomit it.

Let your foot be seldom in your neighbor's house,

lest he have his fill of you and hate you.

Whoever sings songs to a heavy heart

is like one who takes off a garment on a cold day,

and like vinegar on soda.

If your enemy is hungry, give him bread to eat,

and if he is thirsty, give him water to drink,

for you will heap burning coals on his head,

and the LORD will reward you.

PROVERBS 25:16-17, 20-22 ESV

What does it mean? ....
....
....
....
....
....
....
....

How does it make me feel? ....
....
....
....
....
....
....
....

How does it apply to me? ....
....
....
....
....
....
....
....

*P*erfume and incense bring joy to the heart,

and the pleasantness of a friend springs from their heartfelt advice.

Do not forsake your friend or a friend of your family,

and do not go to your relative's house when disaster strikes you—

better a neighbor nearby than a relative far away.

The prudent see danger and take refuge,

but the simple keep going and pay the penalty.

As iron sharpens iron,

so one person sharpens another.

The crucible for silver and the furnace for gold,

but people are tested by their praise.

PROVERBS 27:9-10, 12, 17, 21 NIV

What does it mean? ....
....
....
....
....
....
....

How does it make me feel? ....
....
....
....
....
....
....

How does it apply to me? ....
....
....
....
....
....
....

*T*he wicked flee when no one pursues,

but the righteous are bold as a lion.

Because of the transgression of a land, many are its princes;

but by a man of understanding and knowledge

right will be prolonged.

Evil men do not understand justice,

but those who seek the LORD understand all.

Better is the poor who walks in his integrity

than one perverse in his ways, though he be rich.

One who turns away his ear from hearing the law,

even his prayer is an abomination.

PROVERBS 28:1-2, 5-6, 9 NKJV

What does it mean? ....

....

....

....

....

....

....

....

How does it make me feel? ....

....

....

....

....

....

....

....

How does it apply to me? ....

....

....

....

....

....

....

....

*T*he righteous considereth the cause of the poor:

but the wicked regardeth not to know it.

Scornful men bring a city into a snare:

but wise men turn away wrath.

A fool uttereth all his mind:

but a wise man keepeth it in till afterwards.

Where there is no vision, the people perish:

but he that keepeth the law, happy is he.

The fear of man bringeth a snare:

but whoso putteth his trust in the LORD shall be safe.

PROVERBS 29:7-8, 11, 18, 25 KJV

What does it mean?

How does it make me feel?

How does it apply to me?

When the just are triumphant,

there is great rejoicing,

but when the wicked rise up, people hide.

He who conceals his sins will not succeed;

he who confesses and abandons them will gain mercy.

He who farms his land will have plenty of food,

but he who follows futilities will have plenty of poverty.

A trustworthy person will receive many blessings,

but one rushing to get rich will not go unpunished.

PROVERBS 28:12-13, 19-20 CJB

What does it mean? ....
....
....
....
....
....
....

How does it make me feel? ....
....
....
....
....
....
....

How does it apply to me? ....
....
....
....
....
....
....

*E*very word of God proves true;

he is a shield to those who take refuge in him.

Two things I ask of you;

deny them not to me before I die:

Remove far from me falsehood and lying;

give me neither poverty nor riches;

feed me with the food that is needful for me,

lest I be full and deny you

and say, "Who is the LORD?"

or lest I be poor and steal

and profane the name of my God.

PROVERBS 30:5, 7–9 ESV